This Drawing Book Belongs To:

Ultimate Journals and Notebooks

Made in the USA
Las Vegas, NV
15 October 2024

96724463R00083